For:_____

Let us learn together what is good.

Job 34:4

From:_____

For My Teacher

Copyright 1999 by ZondervanPublishingHouse

ISBN 0-310-97814-9

Requests for information should be addressed to:

ZondervanPublishingHouse
Mail Drop B20
Grand Rapids, Michigan 49530
http://www.zondervan.com

Senior Editor: Gwen Ellis
Project Editor: Pat Matuszak
Designer: Mark Veldheer
Cover Illustration: Johnna Bandle

Printed in Hong Kong

99 00 01 /HK/ 3 2 1

She speaks with wisdom,
and faithful instruction is on her
tongue.

Proverbs 31:26

To those who know Thee not, no
words can paint!
And those who know Thee, know all
words are faint!

Hannah Moore

The Lord is my helper;
I will not be afraid.

Hebrews 13:6

Have courage for the great sorrows of life, and patience for the small ones. When you have laboriously accomplished your daily tasks, go to sleep in peace. God is awake.

Victor Hugo

How great is the love the
Father has lavished on
us, that we should be
called children of God!

1 John 3:1

Our questions and cries powerfully move the Almighty. He parts heaven and shakes earth to respond. He reaches down. He takes hold. Jesus is God's embrace, his way of reaching down and taking hold. Jesus is where we encounter him.

Joni Eareckson Tada

Do not forget the things your eyes have seen or let them slip from your heart as long as you live. Teach them to your children and to their children after them.

Deuteronomy 4:9

Learn to set aside what you see
and hear in order to see and hear
what God would pour out upon
you from his invisible kingdom.

Saint Teresa of Avila

In everything, by prayer and petition, with thanksgiving, present your requests to God.

Philippians 4:6

Spread out your petition before God, and then say, "Thy will, not mine, be done." The sweetest lesson I have learned in God's school is to let the Lord choose for me.

Dwight L. Moody

A heart at peace gives life to the body.

Proverbs 14:30

I can do everything through
Christ who gives me strength.

Philippians 4:13

The greater part of our happiness or
misery depends on our dispositions,
and not on our circumstances.

Martha Washington

Love one another deeply,
from the heart.

1 Peter 1:22

Those who love deeply never grow old; they may die of old age, but they die young.

Benjamin Franklin

God is love. Whoever lives in love lives in God, and God in him.

1 John 4:16

The happiness of life is made up of minute fractions —
a kiss or smile, a kind look, a heartfelt compliment.

William Scott

Whatever you do, work at it with all your heart, as working for the Lord.

Colossians 3:23

If your heart were sincere and upright, every creature would be unto you a looking-glass of life and a book of holy doctrine.

Thomas Á Kempis

The peace of God, which transcends all understanding, will guard your hearts and your minds in Christ Jesus.

Philippians 4:7

A habit of devout fellowship
with God is the spring of all our
life, and the strength of it.

Henry Edward Manning

As for God, his way is perfect; the word of the LORD is flawless. He is a shield for all who take refuge in him.

2 Samuel 22:31

The justice of God must be vast like His compassion. . . . By faith we know His existence; in glory we shall know His nature.

Blaise Pascal

The LORD will guide you always;
he will satisfy your needs in a
sun-scorched land . . . . You
will be like a well-watered garden.

Isaiah 58:11

Thy love is such I can no way repay.
The heavens reward Thee manifold, I
pray.

Anne Bradstreet

Show me your ways, O Lᴏʀᴅ,
teach me your paths.

Psalm 25:4

Have thy heart in heaven and thy hands upon the earth. Ascend in piety and descend in charity. For this is the nature of light and the way of the children.

Thomas Vaughan

The Lord loves righteousness and
justice;
the earth is full of his unfailing
love.

Psalm 33:5

Give God's love away with joy in your heart. No strings attached.

Barbara Johnson

Wisdom is more precious than
rubies,
and nothing you desire can
compare with her.

Proverbs 8:11

A book is a garden, an orchard, a storehouse, a party, a company by the way, a counselor, a multitude of counselors.

Henry Ward Beecher

The fear of the LORD is the beginning
of wisdom;
all who follow his precepts have
good understanding.

Psalm 111:10

Our humanity is a poor thing, except
for the divinity that stirs within us.

Francis Bacon

The wisdom that comes from heaven is first of all pure; then peace-loving, considerate, submissive, full of mercy and good fruit, impartial and sincere.

James 3:17

One who knows how to show
and to accept kindness will be a
friend better than any possession.

Sophocles

Dear friends, now we are children of God, and what we will be has not yet been made known. But we know that when he appears, we shall be like him, for we shall see him as he is.

1 John 3:2

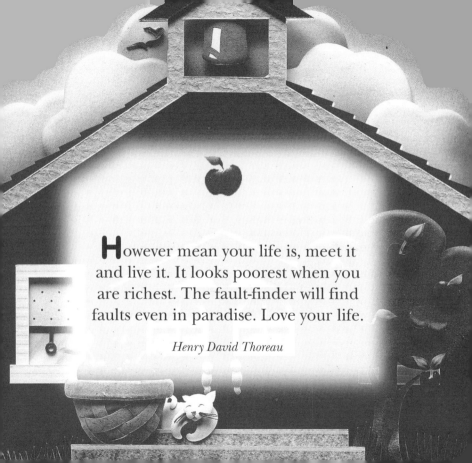

However mean your life is, meet it and live it. It looks poorest when you are richest. The fault-finder will find faults even in paradise. Love your life.

Henry David Thoreau

The LORD gives wisdom,
and from his mouth come
knowledge and understanding.

Proverbs 2:6

The trouble with the world is not that people know too little, but that they know so many things that ain't so.

Mark Twain

If anything is excellent or praiseworthy — think about such things.

Philippians 4:8

When one door of happiness closes, another opens; but often we look so long at the closed door that we do not see the one which has been opened for us.

Helen Keller

Let the word of Christ dwell in you richly as you teach and admonish one another with all wisdom, and as you sing psalms, hymns and spiritual songs with gratitude in your hearts to God.

Colossians 3:16

Gratitude is the heart's memory.

French proverb

Let love and faithfulness never leave you;
write them on the tablet of your heart.

Proverbs 3:3

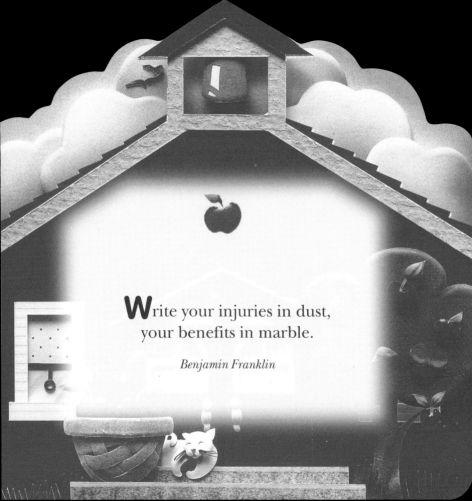

Write your injuries in dust,
your benefits in marble.

Benjamin Franklin

Clothe yourselves with compassion, kindness, humility, gentleness and patience. Bear with each other.

Colossians 3:12–13

If you want to be happy for a year, plant a garden. If you want to be happy for life, plant a tree.

English proverb

May the Lord direct your hearts into
God's love and Christ's perseverance.

2 Thessalonians 3:5

How far that little candle throws his beams!
So shines a good deed in a naughty world.

Shakespeare

We know that in all things God works for the good of those who love him.

Romans 8:28

Troubles are often the tools by which
God fashions us for better things.

Henry Ward Beecher

The wise in heart are called discerning.

Proverbs 16:21

Our Lord does not care so much
for the importance of our works as
for the love with which they are done.

Saint Teresa of Avila

If you spend yourselves . . . .
then your light will rise in the
darkness.

Isaiah 58:10

More things are wrought by prayer
than this world dreams of. . . . .
Let thy voice rise like a fountain.

Alfred Lord Tennyson

Jesus said, "Surely I am with you always, to the very end of the age."

Matthew 28:20

I am only one, but still I am one. I cannot do everything, but still I can do something.

Helen Keller

Imitate those who through
faith and patience inherit
what has been promised.

Hebrews 6:12

The things we do today—
sowing seeds, or sharing simple
truths of Christ—people will someday
refer to as the first things that
prompted them to think of Him.

George Matheson

Guide me in your truth and teach me,
for you are God my Savior,
and my hope is in you all day long.

Psalm 25:5

When we work, we work.
When we pray, God works.

J. Hudson Taylor

Commit to the LORD whatever you do,
and your plans will succeed.

Proverbs 16:3

We must wait on Him moment by moment for the fulfillment of His promised blessings, and must trust Him to obtain them for us. The Spirit must make intercession in us.

Hannah Whitall Smith

We are God's workmanship, created in Christ Jesus to do good works, which God prepared in advance for us to do.

Ephesians 2:10

Allow your life to burst forth,
reaching toward the unseen, the
eternal and the heavenly.

Mrs. Charles Cowman

Create in me a pure heart, O God,
and renew a steadfast spirit within
me. . .
Restore to me the joy of your salvation
and grant me a willing spirit, to
sustain me.

Psalm 51:10,12

There is a need to pray throughout the world, every hour, without ceasing.

Martin Luther

Just as you received Christ Jesus as Lord, continue to live in him, rooted and built up in him, strengthened in the faith as you were taught.

Colossians 2:6–7

In prayer, we are confronted with the important difference between doing works *for* God, and doing the works *of* God. In this sense, it is not like a building project, so much as a garden.

Brad Long

Dear friends, since God so loved us,
we also ought to love one another.

1 John 4:11

One word frees us of all the weight and pain of life; that word is love.

Sophocles

Let us not become weary in doing good, for at the proper time we will reap a harvest if we do not give up.

Galatians 6:9

Kind words toward those you daily meet,
Kind words and actions right,
Will make this life of ours most sweet,
Turn darkness into light.

Isaac Watts

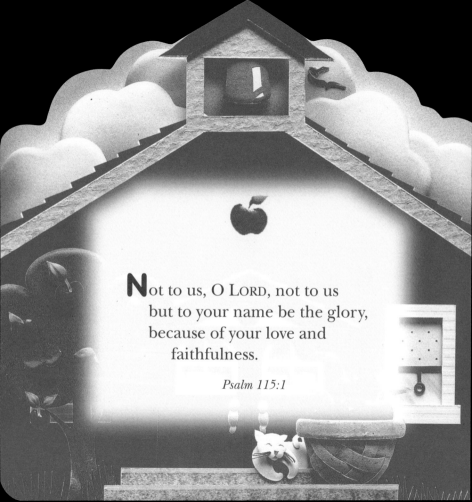

Not to us, O Lord, not to us
but to your name be the glory,
because of your love and
faithfulness.

Psalm 115:1

He that is down, needs fear no fall;
He that is low, no pride;
He that is humble ever shall
Have God to be his guide.

John Bunyan

Praise the LORD, all you nations;
extol him, all you peoples.
For great is his love toward us,
and the faithfulness of the LORD
endures forever.

Psalm 117:1–2

No people on earth have more cause to be thankful than ours. This is said reverently, in no spirit of boastfulness in our own strength, but with gratitude to the Giver of Good who has blessed.

Theodore Roosevelt

God has said, "Never will I leave you; never will I forsake you."

Hebrews 13:5

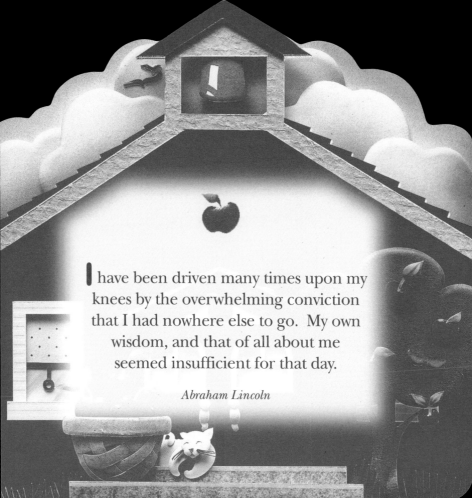

I have been driven many times upon my knees by the overwhelming conviction that I had nowhere else to go. My own wisdom, and that of all about me seemed insufficient for that day.

Abraham Lincoln

I will sing of the LORD's great love
forever;
with my mouth I will make your
faithfulness known through all
generations.

Psalm 89:1

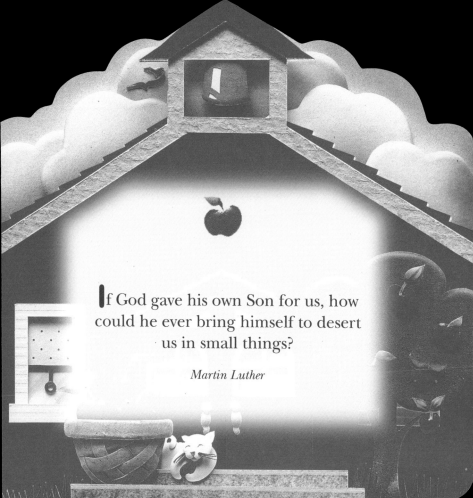

If God gave his own Son for us, how could he ever bring himself to desert us in small things?

Martin Luther

God will not forget your work
and the love you have shown him
as you have helped his people.

Hebrews 6:10

We find rest in those we love,
and we provide a resting place in
ourselves for those who love us.

Bernard of Clairvaux

Live a life of love, just as Christ loved us and gave himself up for us.

Ephesians 5:2

To love is to give one's time. We never give the impression that we care when we are in a hurry.

Paul Tournier

Happiness does not depend on outward things, but on the way we see them.

Leo Tolstoy

Follow the way of love.

1 Corinthians 14:1

Have a heart that never hardens, a temper that never tires, and a touch that never hurts.

Charles Dickens

You gain strength, courage, and
confidence by every experience in
which you really stop to look fear in
the face. . . . . You must do the
thing you think you cannot do.

Eleanor Roosevelt

In all these things we are more than conquerors through Christ who loved us.

Romans 8:37

But come, sweet Hope, from thy divine
retreat,
Come to my breast, and chase my cares away,
Bring calm Content to gild my gloomy seat,
And cheer my bosom with her heav'nly ray.

Phillis Wheatley

Jesus said, "Let the little children come to me, and do not hinder them, for the kingdom of heaven belongs to such as these."

Matthew 19:14

We win by tenderness; we
conquer by forgiveness.

Frederick William Robertson

Let us draw near to God with a sincere
heart in full assurance of faith.

Hebrews 10:22

Grant that we may not so much seek
to be understood as to understand.

Saint Francis of Assisi

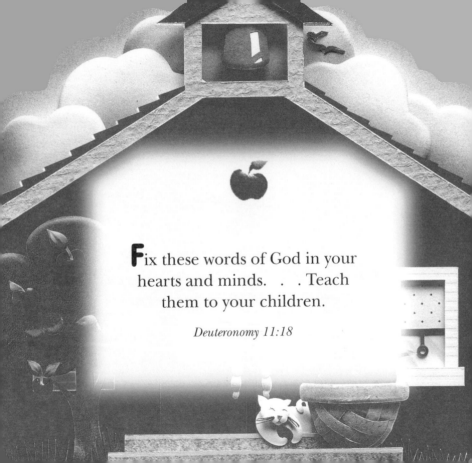

Fix these words of God in your hearts and minds. . . Teach them to your children.

Deuteronomy 11:18

The Bible is God's chart for you to steer by, to keep you from the bottom of the sea, and to show you where the harbour is, and how to reach it without running on rocks and bars.

Henry Ward Beecher

Man looks at the outward appearance, but the LORD looks at the heart.

1 Samuel 16:7

The greatest good you can do for another is not just to share your riches, but to reveal to him his own.

Benjamin Disraeli

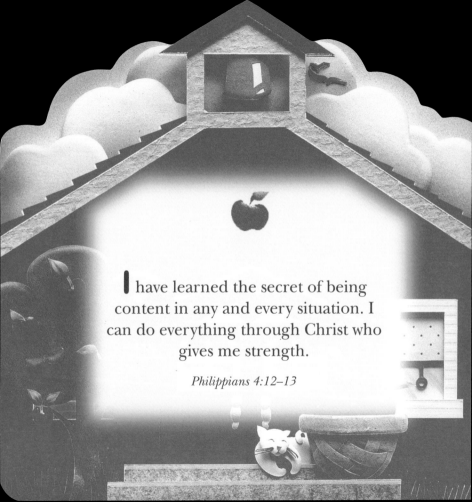

I have learned the secret of being content in any and every situation. I can do everything through Christ who gives me strength.

Philippians 4:12–13

What lies behind us and what lies before us are tiny matters, compared to what lies within us.

Ralph Waldo Emerson

May the words of my mouth and the
meditation of my heart
be pleasing in your sight,
O LORD, my Rock and my
Redeemer.

Psalm 19:14

The word *trust* is the heart of faith.
Trust sees and feels, and it leans
on those who have a great, living,
and genuine heart of love.

Mrs. Charles Cowman

Find rest, O my soul, in God alone;
  my hope comes from him.
He alone is my rock and my salvation;
  he is my fortress, I will not be
    shaken.

Psalm 62:5–6

God can use adversities in our lives to strengthen our faith and make us strong, mature believers. He can take the broken pieces of our sorrow and make something beautiful and meaningful.

Hope MacDonald

Jesus said, "Whoever drinks the water I give him will never thirst. Indeed, the water I give him will become in him a spring of water welling up to eternal life."

John 4:14

We cannot live in a vacuum. We
have to express our being by creating.
Creativity follows being.

Ingrid Trobisch

Keep on loving each other.

Hebrews 13:1

When we let God's life flow through us, his Spirit will grow and nourish everyone around us.

Barbara Johnson

Let us hold unswervingly to the hope we profess, for God who promised is faithful.

Hebrews 10:23

In God's economy. . . weakness is strength. The last shall be first. The foolish things of the world God uses to confound the wise.

Cal Thomas

Every good and perfect gift is
from above, coming down from the
Father of the heavenly lights.

James 1:17

The Spirit of God first imparts
love; he next inspires hope,
and then gives liberty.

Dwight L. Moody

Now we see but a poor reflection as in a mirror; then we shall see face to face. Now I know in part; then I shall know fully, even as I am fully known.

1 Corinthians 13:12

Who has seen the wind?
Neither you nor I:
But when the trees bow down their
       heads,
The wind is passing by.

Christina Rossetti

Let your conversation be
always full of grace.

Colossians 4:6

My call is to be a light wherever God sends me. I believe he sent me here to be a light to many people who would never go to a church. I don't want to hide away from the world, cloistered away with others who believe exactly as I do.

Connie Neal

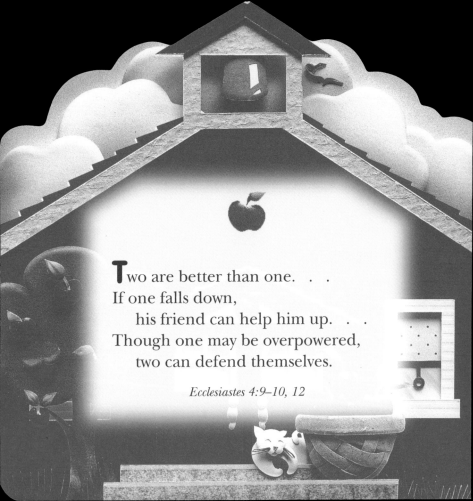

Two are better than one. . .
If one falls down,
   his friend can help him up. . .
Though one may be overpowered,
   two can defend themselves.

Ecclesiastes 4:9–10, 12

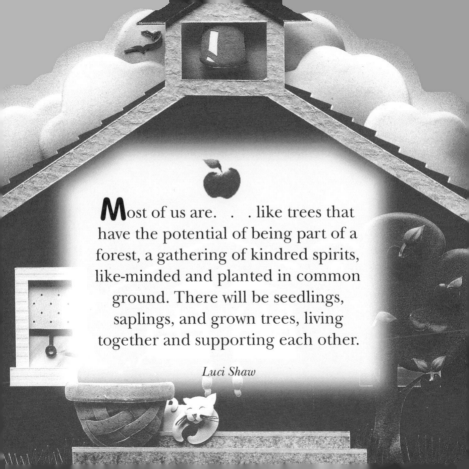

Most of us are. . . like trees that have the potential of being part of a forest, a gathering of kindred spirits, like-minded and planted in common ground. There will be seedlings, saplings, and grown trees, living together and supporting each other.

Luci Shaw

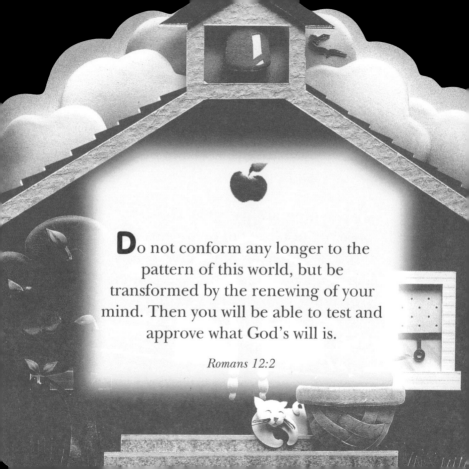

Do not conform any longer to the pattern of this world, but be transformed by the renewing of your mind. Then you will be able to test and approve what God's will is.

Romans 12:2

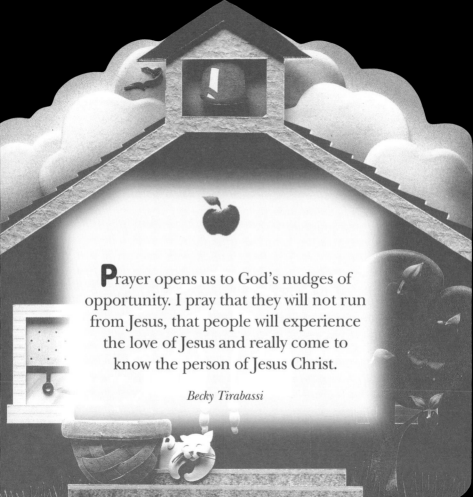

Prayer opens us to God's nudges of opportunity. I pray that they will not run from Jesus, that people will experience the love of Jesus and really come to know the person of Jesus Christ.

Becky Tirabassi

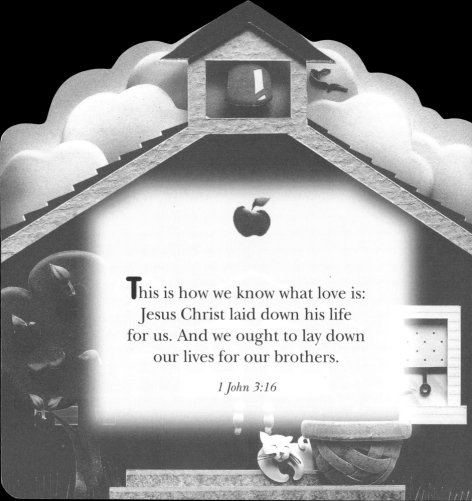

This is how we know what love is:
Jesus Christ laid down his life
for us. And we ought to lay down
our lives for our brothers.

1 John 3:16

Strengthening one another with the true hope Jesus offers is one of the most important things we can do. We can do this in many little ways that make a difference.

Jan Dravecky

Sources

Becky Tirabassi, *Wild Things Happen When I Pray* (Grand Rapids: Zondervan 1994).

Connie Neal, *Dancing in the Arms of God* (Grand Rapids: 1994).

Luci Shaw, *Water My Soul* (Grand Rapids: Zondervan 1994).

Hope MacDonald, *When Angels Appear* (Grand Rapids: Zondervan 1994).

Jan Dravecky, *Stand by Me* (Grand Rapids: Zondervan 1994).

Brad Long, *Prayer That Shapes the Future* (Grand Rapids: Zondervan 1994).

Cal Thomas, *Blinded by Might* (Grand Rapids: Zondervan 1994).

Ingrid Trobisch, *The Confident Woman* (New York:HarperCollins 1993).